THE WELSH HIGHLAND RAILWAY

Alun Turner

Revised Edition 1996

Welsh Highland Railway Limited

THE WELSH HIGHLAND RAILWAY

This edition ©1996 Alun Turner & the Welsh Highland Railway Limited

Author:
Alun Turner

Book design, Cover Artwork & Drawings by:
Roy C. Link, 1 Station Cottages, Harling Road,
East Harling, Norwich, Norfolk, NR16 2QP.

Printed in Great Britain by:
Amadeus Press Limited, 517 Leeds Road,
Huddersfield, West Yorkshire, HD2 1YJ.

Published by:
Welsh Highland Railway Ltd.

Distributed by:
Cwmni Rheilffordd Beddgelert Cyf.

ISBN 0950 1178 4 6

PREFACE TO REVISED EDITION

The original edition of this book was published in 1990 as "A history of the Welsh Highland Railway, Part 1, 1864 to 1948". Alun Turner intended it to be a popular history and it has been a regular and steady seller. In issuing this revised edition, the opportunity has been taken to make some amendments and revisions and to include a small amount of new material and photographs.

The story since 1948 is summarised in Chapter 5. The sequence of events from the formation of the original Welsh Highland Railway Society in 1961 to the present day will in the future make a fascinating and intriguing story of frustrated ambitions, political deviousness and eventual success. The historian with a sense of irony, may well see the events of the last thirty five years as merely a continuation of the same story since the grandiose schemes of the North Wales Narrow Gauge Railway Company and others were originally conceived in the 1870s.

For all those interested in the history of the Welsh Highland Railway and its predecessors we hope that this new edition will prove to be a useful introduction and a firm foundation for further reading and research.

Nick Booker
Chairman
Welsh Highland Railway Development Team
Porthmadog
July 1996

AUTHOR'S PREFACE

Some may consider it extravagant to put the date of 1864 to 1948 to the history of the line that only ran originally from 1923 until 1937. However the history of the Welsh Highland Railway cannot be considered on its own, one has to consider the part played by two of its fore-runners, the Croesor Tramway and the North Wales Narrow Gauge Railways, for without the existence of these two lines it is doubtful whether the Welsh Highland Railway would ever have come into being. Certainly there were enough attempts which failed to link these two lines as this book will try to relate. Would someone have tried to build a through route and, more importantly, have succeeded without them? I feel it is exceedingly doubtful. So the date of 1864 is, I feel, valid.

As for the later date, well, the Welsh Highland Railway is very much alive and kicking in its re-incarnation as the Welsh Highland Light Railway (1964) Ltd., which is dedicated to restoring the line.

Some words of explanation are necessary to those reading this book. I have attempted to simplify the history of the enterprises prior to the Welsh Highland Railways formation. This book is intended for those who wish to know more about the Welsh Highland Railway without getting involved with all the various Acts of Parliament and goings on behind the scenes in the years prior to 1923, although some of this material is essential to understanding and has been included. Some place names have changed their spelling several times in the period this book covers and so to save confusion Carnarvon, Caernarvon, Carnarfon and Caernarfon is always referred to as Caernarfon and others remain standard, if not current, throughout.

Alun Turner.
April 1990.

ACKNOWLEDGMENTS

The publishers wish to thank Alun Turner who has kindly agreed to the issue of this new edition. The original edition of the book was produced with the assistance and encouragement of David Allan, John Keylock and Michael Seymour.

Andrew Neale of Plateway Press has revised the text, selected the photographs and managed the production of the new edition with the assistance and encouragement of David Allan, Miv & Les Blackwell, Nick Booker, Eluned Jones, John Keylock and Pauline Weatherby.

The publishers thank the copyright holders of the photographs used and these are credited where known.

A number of books and other publications were consulted during the preparation of both the original and revised editions of this book. Some of the more key sources to which the interested reader may wish to refer are shown below.

BIBLIOGRAPHY

Narrow Gauge Railways in North Wales by Charles E. Lee
Narrow Gauge Railways in South Caernarvonshire by J.I.C. Boyd
The Welsh Highland Railway by Charles E. Lee
More about the Welsh Highland Railway by Various.
The Festiniog Railway by J.I.C. Boyd
Introducing Russell by Peter Deegan
History of Caernarvonshire by A.H. Dodd
Madocks and the Wonder of Wales by E. Beazely
Snowdonia by Various
Russell: The Story of a Locomotive by Alun Turner
Russell: The Story of an Historic Narrow Gauge Steam locomotive by Andrew Neale.

CONTENTS

| | Page |

Preface to revised edition iii

Author's Preface iii

Acknowledgments & Bibliography iv

Chapter One
The Predecessors 1

Chapter Two
The Welsh Highland Railway 15

Chapter Three
The Route Described 27

Chapter Four
Working the Line - A Memoir 35

Chapter Five
The Story Since 1948 - a summary 41

THIS BOOK IS DEDICATED
TO ALL MEMBERS, PAST AND PRESENT,
OF THE WELSH HIGHLAND LIGHT RAILWAY (1964) Ltd.

*May the dream
one day become reality.*

CHAPTER ONE
THE FORERUNNERS

Dinas Junction Station, 1925. MOEL TRYFAN and Welsh Highland train pose with an L.M.S. up train headed by a Webb "Cauliflower" goods loco on the right.
(C.J.Keylock collection).

The Welsh Highland Railway was formed by the linking of two much earlier railways, the North Wales Narrow Gauge Railways and the Croesor Tramway, by a new line between South Snowdon (Rhyd - ddu) and Croesor Junction, some 8¼ miles in length. It is therefore necessary when considering the history of the Welsh Highland Railway to start with the history of those two lines and others which associated with them.

The Croesor Tramway was the first of these to be built, being officially opened on the 1st August 1864, although evidence exists of traffic over part of the line for up to twelve months earlier. The line was built by Hugh Beaver Roberts as a private undertaking constructed under wayleave. Of 1 ft.11 inches gauge, the line ran from Porthmadoc, where it had sidings on the quayside and later, a trans-shipment siding with the Cambrian Coast line, to the upper end of the Croesor Valley, a distance of approximately 6 miles although this was described officially in returns as 4½, and even just 1¼ miles. Built to serve the slate quarries in the Croesor Valley, it was goods carrying only although in 1864 an application was made to Parliament "To provide for the maintenance and use by the public of the existing railway made by Hugh Beaver Roberts of Plas Llanddoget which commences near the rock or place known as Carreg Hylldrem in a certain field called Cae Ochor Rhainwal, part of the

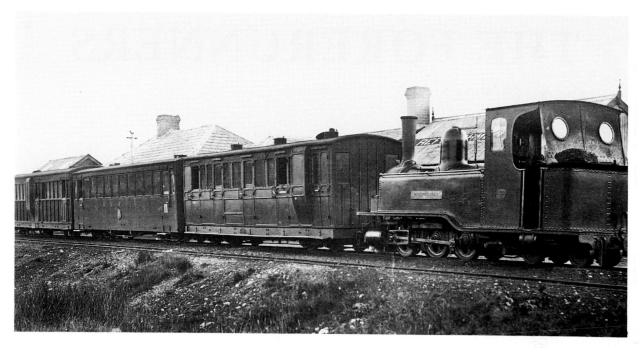

Above: MOEL TRYFAN poses with a mixed train of passenger stock at Rhyd-ddu Station about 1910. From right to left are the Guard's composite, corridor composite, Gloucester 6-wheeler and 'workman's' coach.

Below: MOEL TRYFAN's driver proudly poses with his locomotive at the passenger platform at Dinas Junction about 1905. Note the prominent brake reservoir under the cab.
(Both: Locomotive Publishing Co.)

Welsh Highland Rly.

BEDDGELERT leads a double headed train at Dinas about 1892 with almost all the N.W.N.G.Rly. carriage stock at that time, including three small four wheeled coaches.
(W.H.R. collection).

farm called Park and terminates at or near Ynys Carrigduon at Porthmadoc in the parish of Ynyscyhaiarn, together with station sidings and works and to adapt and use for passengers as well as other traffic."

Royal Assent was given to the bill on the 5th July 1865. It is interesting to note that although the gauge was stated as 2ft. powers were given to increase this to 3ft., on application to the Board of Trade. The bill also incorporated the tramway as the Croesor and Porthmadoc Railway Company. By a statuary mortgage dated 23rd June 1870 the Company mortgaged its undertaking to Mary Elizabeth Littledale for £8000 at 5.½% interest.

The construction of the tramway was of 20 lb. per yard wrought iron rails laid in chairs on timber sleepers. Because of the lightness of the construction it was only suitable for horse or gravity working and had the railway gone forward with its powers under the Act of 5th July 1865 it would, presumably, have had to relay the line within little more than two years of its building. In fact Charles Easton Spooner, the Engineer of the Ffestiniog Railway, prepared an estimate for the proposed work - some £14,960.

The line was to remain horse-drawn until re-laid to become part of the Welsh Highland Railway and even then the part of the line from Croesor Junction to the quarries in the Croesor Valley remained horse-drawn although on occasions a farm tractor would haul wagons along the line. Unusually, for a horse-drawn line, the tramway never owned its own horses but hired them from neighbouring farms.

Linked with the Croesor Tramway at Porthmadoc was the Gorseddau Junction and Porthmadoc Railway which joined up with the Croesor Tramway by Porthmadoc Flour Mill (Now the Pottery).

Originally a 3ft gauge line and known as the Tremadoc Tramway, it ran along the side of Y Cyt (Today reverted to its original use as a land drain but once in use as a canal capable of handling ships of up to 120 tons) and served an Ironstone mine at Llidiart Yspytty. It is a possibility that the Tremadoc Tramway actually pre-dated the Ffestiniog Railway in the Area, for it is shown on maps dated 1846 and is impossible to put a date of opening to the Tremadoc Tramway. In 1856 the Bangor and Pothmadoc Slate and Slate Slab Co. Ltd., came to an arrangement with the owners of the Tremadoc line and built an extension to the Gorsedddau Quarries to provide a convenient outlet for the slate from the quarry to the quay at Porthmadoc. The line was converted to 2ft. gauge in 1878 and it was at this time that the link with the Croesor Tramway was made. The line was mostly gravity and horse-drawn although it did own a DeWinton vertically boilered locomotive for a time.

The use of the 2ft. line was short lived and had ceased by 1892. Parts of the trackbed are still recognizable in Portmadoc today, particularly in the embankment that runs alongside Y Cyt along Madoc Street, and the stile crossing at the rear of the present day Welsh Highland Railways car park is the site of the Tramways crossing of the Cambrian Coastline. But the most spectacular remains are the roofless shell of Ynyspandy Slate Mill, near Cwm Ystradlyn, now under the protection of the National Trust.

The North Wales Narrow Gauge Railways brought forward a scheme which covered almost all the route eventually covered by the Welsh Highland Railway and, in its initial concept, quite considerably more. The scheme stemmed from the success that the introduction of steam traction and regular passenger carrying services had brought to the Ffestiniog Railway and proposed originally to build a narrow gauge network in North West Wales to link most of the larger towns. In brief this involved extending the Croesor Tramway from Croesor Junction through Beddgelert and Capel Curig to Bettws-y-Coed and thence on by a branch which would split to reach both Corwen and Penmachno. A further line would run from Porthdinllaen through Pwllheli and then alongside the Cambrian Coast line to Portmadoc to link up there with the Southern end of the Croesor Tramway. As an alternative it proposed for a third rail to be added to the Cambrian Coast line so that the line could serve both gauges. Hardly surprisingly both these proposals were opposed by the Cambrian owners. A further line would run from Dinas, (3 miles south of Caernarfon) where it would share the station on the L.N.W.R.'s Bangor to Afon Wen line, to Rhyd-ddu with a branch line leaving the main line at Tryfan Junction and running to Bryngwyn with an incline at the end to serve the slate quarries in the Moel Tryfan area.

In the event applications were made to Parliament only for the line from Croesor Junction to Bettws-Y-Coed and from Dinas to Rhyd-ddu and the branch to Bryngwyn. These were duly approved and the North Wales Narrow Gauge Railways Company was incorporated by Act of Parliament on the 6th August 1872. The two approved railways were to be known as the General Undertaking and the Moel Tryfan Undertaking respectively. Both capitals and income of the two undertakings were to be kept distinctly separate. Charles Easton Spooner was appointed Engineer of the new Company.

The General Undertaking, the proposed 23 mile line from Croesor Junction to Bettws-Y-Coed, was never built and the Company sought and obtained an Act of Parliament dated 13th July 1876 allowing it to abandon this venture. The idea was not forgotten however and in November 1903 the North Wales Power & Traction Co. Ltd., obtained a Light Railway Order for a line from Beddgelert to Bettws-Y-Coed but again no work was ever started and the powers lapsed in 1907. These powers were then acquired by the Porthmadoc, Beddgelert and South Snowdon Railway (about which more later) who also let them lapse and with that the scheme faded into oblivion.

The Moel Tryfan Undertaking, to construct a line of 5½ miles in length from Dinas to Bryngwyn and a line of 7¼ miles in length from the former line at Tryfan Junction to Rhyd-Ddu was the part of the scheme the directors devoted their attention to.

It is interesting to note that in the original Act and in all communications prior to opening it is the Bryngwyn line that is referred to as the main line and the Rhyd-Ddu line as the branch. Subsequent to opening the position was reversed and the Dinas to Rhyd-Ddu line became the main line.

A prospectus was issued on the 23rd January 1873 with regard to the authorised capital of £66,000, by which time a contract had already been made with

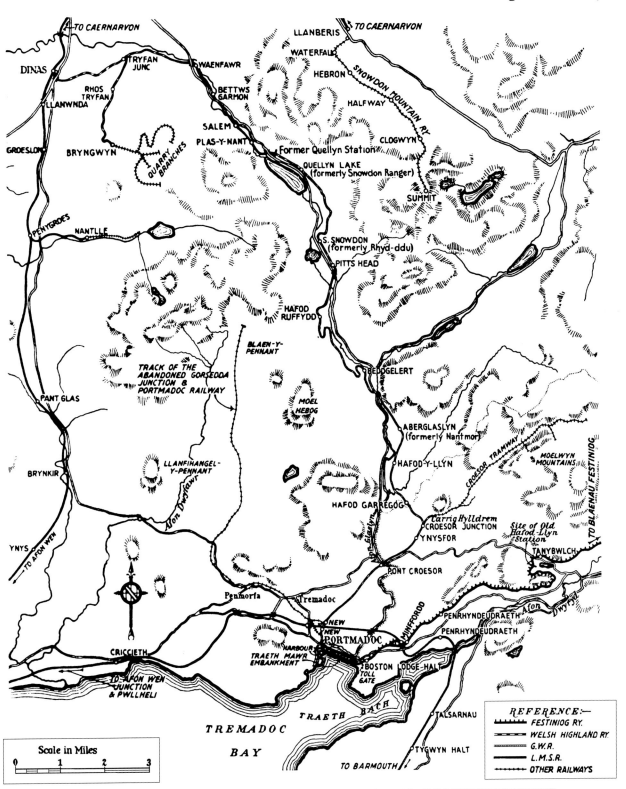

THE WELSH HIGHLAND RAILWAY & ITS CONSTITUENTS

BEDDGELERT at Dinas about 1905. The shorter chimney probably dates from her rebuild at the builder's works in 1894. (Locomotive Publishing Co.)

Hugh Unsworth M'Kie of Tremadoc for the construction of the line and an agreement dated 23rd December 1872 had been entered into with the same Hugh Beaver Roberts who had been the instigator of the Croesor Tramway, to lease the Moel Tryfan lines for 21 years from their completion. This agreement was slightly modified in April 1873 and sanctioned by Parliament in an Act which received Royal Approval on the 16th June 1873.

Difficulties arose very early with the contractor overpayment for work and in August 1874 Roberts repudiated the lease. The unsteady financial state of the Company forced it to avoid lengthy and expensive litigation to enforce the lease. Surprisingly, despite its precarious financial state, the Railway considered building a further line in 1875 when C.E. Spooner, then Engineer of both the Ffestiniog Railway and the North Wales Narrow Gauge Railways, proposed a rack railway, similar to the one running from Llanberis, to be built from Rhyd-Ddu to the summit of Snowdon. The argument was that the rack railway would increase passenger traffic over the North Wales Narrow Gauge. But the financial problems caused the scheme to be dropped although it was to re-surface in 1922 when the new Welsh Highland Railway considered building such a line. But after obtaining plans and quotations for a suitable locomotive, the Welsh Highland dropped the idea too. In February 1876 M'Kie surrendered possession of the works and plant and a new contract was entered into with J Boys, who completed all but three miles of the line by the end of 1876.

The sections of the line from Dinas to Bryngwyn and from Tryfan Junction to Lake Quellyn were opened for goods traffic on the 21st May 1877 and passenger traffic commenced on the 15th August that year. A further ¾ mile section between Lake Quellyn and Snowdon Ranger was brought into service on the 1st June 1878 and the remaining 2 miles from Snowdon Ranger to Rhyd-Ddu opened on the 14th

Welsh Highland Rly.

Vulcan Foundry 0-6-4T SNOWDON RANGER is seen at Dinas on 23rd. June, 1909.
(Late K.C.A.R.Nunn)

May 1881. The Company's financial problems increased with the opening. The slate trade was suffering a depression at the time and the line worked at a loss from the start. The Company owned none of its rolling stock, hiring it from a contractor who's rentals fell into arrears and on the 13th December 1878 James Cholmeley Russell was appointed by the High Court as Receiver. At this time C.E. Spooner severed his connection with the Railway and James Cleminson became Engineer and Locomotive Superintendent. Despite these problems the Company gained authorization in an Act dated 31st July 1885 to extend the line to Caernarfon Harbour. Presumably it felt that its dependence on the L.N.W.R. at Dinas was the root of its troubles and wished to avoid this dependency.

Five locomotives were built for the North Wales Narrow Gauge Railway. Three of these were of the Single Fairlie type. The Vulcan Foundry built two 0-6-4 Fairlie locomotives, "Snowdon Ranger" and "Moel Tryfan" which carried numbers 739 and 738 respectively from original drawings signed 'C.E.Spooner per G.Percival Spooner' which were completed in*1875 and used to work the main line when it opened in 1877. These two locomotives were very similar in design to the four coupled engine introduced by G.P. Spooner on the Ffestiniog Railway about a year later.

Both were fitted with Stephenson valve gear, cylinders 8½ x 14 ins., side tanks, solid disc wheels 2ft. 6 ins. in diameter and inside bearings throughout. The trailing bogie had 1 ft. 7 ins diameter wheels. The outline was plain and neat, with a stovepipe chimney and a round-topped brass-cased dome carrying a single Salter safety valve on the middle of the boiler barrel, this barrel being 2 ft. ½ inch in diameter and 8ft long between tube plates containing 104 tubes of 1½ inch diameter. The total heating surface was 361·6 sq/ft. The grate area was 6 sq/ft. which gave 60·26 sq/ft. of heating surface per square foot of grate.

Working pressure was 140 lb. per sq. inch. The power bogie was pivoted under a cast iron saddle riveted to the underside of the boiler, and steam was received at the valve chest through a pendulum pipe, pivoted immediately below the smokebox.

Tank capacity was 359 gallons and coal capacity was 10 cwt. The weight of each locomotive in working order was 14.½ tons, of which 10½ tons rested on the six-coupled wheels, and 4 tons on the trailing bogie. The total wheelbase was 14ft 11½ inches, to which the leading bogie contributed 6ft. and the trailing bogie 3 ft. 6 ins.

As built, no continuous brake appears to have been fitted, but both locomotives underwent repairs at the works of Davis & Metcalfe Ltd. of Romiley near Stockport in 1903 and the Westinghouse brake, with which both engines were equipped in their later years, may well have been fitted then. The Westinghouse compressor was installed in the cab, and the reservoirs beneath the footplate on each side of the cab floor. Both locomotives received new boilers and a heavy overhaul during their times at Davis and Metcalfe Ltd.

In 1908 "Snowdon Ranger" was sent to the Hunslet Engine Co.Ltd. of Leeds for repair and "Moel Tryfan" was re-tubed in 1913. By 1917 both locomotives were in very poor condition but the Railway could not afford replacement. The solution was novel although not unique in narrow gauge history; they built a new locomotive out of the best parts of the two engines. This locomotive utilized "Snowdon Ranger's" frames and "Moel Tryfan's" boiler and what they could not use and was not worth keeping as spares was cut up for scrap. This hybrid locomotive retained the name "Moel Tryfan" and continued in service on the main line. In 1924 it was cut down for working through the tunnels on the Ffestiniog Railway. Finally it was taken into the Ffestiniog Boston Lodge Works in 1936 for boiler repair but the work was never carried out. Dismantled some years later, its remains could be seen scattered around the yard until 1955 when the parts were finally scrapped.

For the Bryngwyn branch an outside framed 0-6-4 tank engine built in 1878 by the Hunslet Engine Co. Ltd. and named "Beddgelert" was purchased. It was a larger locomotive than the two Fairlie types and was fitted with a saddle tank, flared top chimney with a polished-brass bell-mouthed casing enclosing the dome and the Salter safety valves. Four squares and boxes were mounted pannier fashion, two on each side of the tank. Legend has it that "Beddgelert" came equipped with a boiler on the incline principle to counteract the ruling gradient of 1 in 39/48 on the Bryngwyn branch. Photographs of "Beddgelert", of which few survive as she seldom worked the main line where most of the photographs of this period were taken, are not clear. The original drawings do not show the boiler to be inclined but all accounts from those who visited the line support the incline theory.

"Beddgelert" had 2 ft. 6 in. coupled wheels and 1 ft 10 in.bogie wheels, 10 x 16 in. cylinders, 416 sq. ft. of heating surface and a grate area of 7·9 sq. ft. The total wheelbase was 15 ft. 11 in., of which 6 ft. 2 in. was rigid. With 450 gallons in the tank the engine weighed 17 tons, of which 12 tons rested on the coupled wheels. The locomotive worked at 160 lbs per square inch boiler pressure.

Until 1906 these locomotives ran all the North Wales Narrow Gauge services. The Fairlies, as already mentioned, were re-built but "Beddgelert" was scrapped in 1906 after a new 2-6-2 tank engine "Russell", built by the Hunslet Engine Co. Ltd.,was acquired. This locomotive was in fact purchased by the Porthmadoc, Beddgelert and South Snowdon Railway especially to run on the North Wales Narrow Gauge. The full circumstances of this unusual purchase will become clearer later in this chapter. Noticeable features of the new locomotive were the Walschaerts valve gear, outside frames and long side tanks. The round topped dome had a bright brass casing and the chimney a flared top. Between the chimney and dome a canister shaped sand box was mounted originally, this was later removed. Cylinders were 10 ¾ x15 ins. the diameter of the coupled wheels was 2 ft. 4 in. the leading and trailing wheels 1 ft. 6 ins. in diameter.The total heating surface was 381 square feet and the grate area 6·25 square feet. The tanks had a capacity of 440 gallons and the engine weighed 20 tons in working order.*

The last engine was obtained in September 1908. It was another single boiler Fairlie type 0-6-4 tank

---

The full story of "Russell", still running on the Welsh Highland Railway today, is to be found in
"RUSSELL - the story of an Historic Narrow Gauge Steam Locomotive", *available from the Welsh Highland Railway Ltd.*

Welsh Highland Rly.

Above: Then almost new, GOWRIE poses for the camera at Rhyd-ddu on 23rd. June, 1909. (Late K.C.A.R.Nunn)
Below: GOWRIE stands in the goods yard at Dinas Junction about 1910. (WH.R. collection)

Rhyd-ddu was later renamed 'Snowdon'. MOEL TYFAN enters with a Portmadoc train.
(W.H.R. collection)

locomotive apparently the last of this type of locomotive to be built for use in the British Isles, built by the Hunslet Engine Co.Ltd.

Originally this locomotive ran un-named but eventually she was named "Gowrie", after Gowrie Colquhoun Aicheson, the Manager of the Porthmadoc, Beddgelert and South Snowdon Railway Co. This engine differed considerably from the two Vulcan Foundry engines in outward appearance. The boiler, 2ft 5 in. in diameter x 8 ft 10 in. long, had a raised round-top firebox and the side tanks stopped short over the driving axle. There was no footplate round the front end and the rear bogie had outside frames. It had 9½ x 14 ins.cylinders, the coupled wheels had a diameter of 2 ft. 4½in. on a wheelbase of 5 ft. 6 ins. The trailing bogie had wheels of 1 ft 10 ins. diameter and the total wheelbase was 14 feet. The boiler contained 65 brass tubes of 1½in. outside diameter providing 252 square feet of heating surface. The copper firebox had a grate area of 5 square feet and a heating surface of 30 square feet. The working pressure was 160 lbs per square inch and steam distribution was by Walschaerts valve gear. The tanks held 400 gallons of water and the bunker capacity was 1 ton 2 cwt. of coal. The weight in working order was 18 tons 10 cwt. of which 11 tons 6 cwt. rested on the coupled wheels.

The North Wales Narrow Gauge painted its locomotives brown (Although some say red-brown and others Midland red) of a similar shade to the old North British Colour, lined out in black and yellow. Carriages had a two colour finish resembling the former Lancashire and Yorkshire Railway. The first passenger coaches were six-wheelers with Cleminson Trucks, as used on the Manx Northern and the Southwold Railways. They were roofed and fully

Welsh Highland Rly.

The bridge to carry the ill-fated Portmadoc, Beddgelert & South Snowdon Railway over the main road south of The Goat Hotel, Beddgelert, was completed but never used and is still a familiar landmark today. This picture was taken during construction about 1910. Note the contractor's temporary railway and V-skips on the embankment.
(W.H.R. collection)

glazed above the waistline, weighing 4½ tons each and 30 feet long, containing seating for 42 passengers. Subsequently the closed compartment or semi-open type of coach was adopted and each compartment seated 8 passengers in the third class and 6 passengers in the first class.

Whilst the North Wales Narrow Gauge was busy working its completed section, various attempts were made to either reach Beddgelert from Portmadoc by utilizing the Croesor Tramway or to provide a through route by linking the North Wales Narrow Gauge and the Croesor Tramway. In 1879 the name of the Croesor and Porthmadoc Railway Company became the Porthmadoc, Croesor & Beddgelert Tram Railway Company and proposed an extension 4 miles long between Llanfrothen and Beddgelert. In 1882 however Mary Littledale secured the appointment of a receiver to this Company as the principal and outstanding interest on her mortgage then amounted to over £10,000. The North Wales Narrow Gauge had in fact beaten the Croesor Tramway into receivership, as previously noted, so that anyone acquiring the two companies could provide a through route from Porthmadoc to Dinas with possible access to Caernarfon.

There was no lack of pretenders to achieve one or both of these objects. Schemes were put forward by the Beddgelert & Rhyd-Ddu Railway. The Porthmadoc, Beddgelert and Rhyd-Ddu Railway. The Porthmadoc, Beddgelert and Snowdon Light Railway. The Caernarvon, Beddgelert & Porthmadoc Railway. The Beddgelert Railway, and the Porthmadoc & Beddgelert Railway. All of these had the object of reaching Beddgelert if not the full through route by a

RUSSELL pauses at Waenfawr with the daily freight train in 1920. By then this was the only traffic on the N.W.N,G.Rly. but despite the near derelict track the locomotive is commendably clean and polished.
(The late C.R.Clinker)

variety of routes and gauges. It was another of these seemingly endless permutations of names of places. The Porthmadoc, Beddgelert and South Snowdon Railway which was to come closest to achieving the through route and was, apart from the Beddgelert Railway, the only one to actually commence building the proposed route.

The Portmadoc, Beddgelert and South Snowdon Railway Co., was incorporated under an Act of Parliament dated 17th August 1901. The Act gave the new Company power to purchase the Croesor Tramway from the Porthmadoc Croesor and Beddgelert Tram Railway Co., and this purchase was made on the 30th June 1901 by the payment of £10,000 to the receiver of the latter Company. James Cholmeley Russell, who was also the receiver of the North Wales Narrow Gauge Railways. The Porthmadoc, Beddgelert and South Snowdon (Henceforth referred to as the P.B. & S.S.) was authorised to construct a railway between Portmadoc and Beddgelert utilizing the Croesor Tramway part of the way. The North Wales Narrow Gauge had already obtained a Light Railway Order on the 3rd November 1900 authorizing it to extend from Rhyd-Ddu to Beddgelert. Thus by purchasing the North Wales Narrow Gauge the P.B. & S.S. could provide the proposed through route. The P.B. & S.S. was further empowered, by an Act of Parliament dated 15th August 1904, to construct a line from Dinas northwards to reach Caernarfon harbour. Although the P.B & S.S. purchased land to this end, no work was ever commenced on this line which would have relieved the North Wales Narrow Gauge Railway's dependence on the L.N.W.R. at Dinas Junction.

Work however, commenced on the extension between Croesor Junction and Rhyd-Ddu although it was sporadic and piecemeal. Part of this work can still be seen today in the Beddgelert area. The rail bridge

Welsh Highland Rly.

Another view of the P.B.S.S.Rly. under construction.
(W.H.R. collection)

across the road leading into Beddgelert from the South and the nearby stone piers formed part of this work but were never used as the Welsh Highland Railway chose a different route out of Beddgelert when it came into being. Across the river from the line of these works, remains of the low embankment built to take the line exist. running to a point just short of where the Welsh Highland Railway track crossed the Glaslyn at Bryn-y-Felin. The P.B. & S.S. bridge across the Glaslyn was purchased but never put into place and was sold off between 1908 and 1912.

It was the P.B. & S.S. who ordered and paid for "Russell" in 1906. With "Beddgelert" worn out and the North Wales Narrow Gauge unable to afford a replacement the P.B. & S.S. were faced with a dilemma. "Beddgelert" was the only locomotive capable of hauling the slate trains on the Bryngwyn branch. Any disruption of services on this line could cause the quarry owners to look for alternative ways of moving their slate, perhaps never to return to the railway. Such loss of revenue would be disastrous to the North Wales Narrow Gauge and to the P.B. & S.S. when they completed their link line and took over the North Wales line. It was under these circumstances that the P.B. & S.S. took the unusual step of purchasing a locomotive to run on a line they did not own.

Use of the North Wales Narrow Gauge declined from 1897 when the tonnage of slate carried had peaked and the passenger traffic also started declining from 1908 when the railway faced increasing competition from road transport. The outbreak of the First World War in 1914 further hit demand as tourist traffic almost ceased. At this time passenger trains were cut to three trains daily each way. On the 31st October 1916 even this service was suspended, although the announcement of this added that it was hoped to resume full services at the end of the war.

However, with the end of the war in 1918 there was no resumption of passenger services and the line remained goods only.

With the reduction of services in 1916 "Gowrie" and "Russell" were more than sufficient to handle the demands of the line, now reduced to four trains per week on the Bryngwyn branch and trains only running on the main line to Rhyd-Ddu on an "as required" basis, mainly carrying coal and small goods. With the re-building of "Moel Tryfan", the opportunity was taken of selling "Gowrie". Whether this was because as the newest of the locomotives she would fetch the best price or whether because she was, by repute, less than satisfactory in operation is unknown. Whatever the reason "Gowrie" was sold to the British Government in 1918 (Although others have put this date as 1915, which is unlikely) Details of its service or its new owners are unknown but in 1919 she turned up in Wakes Geneva Yard in Darlington and in 1922 she was to be found working on an Aerodrome contract at Marske on Sea, near Redcar. She was advertised for sale in 1928 at the end of this contract and no further trace of her has ever been found.

By 1911 the P.B. & S.S. had all but totally abandoned their plans. The various local authorities interested themselves in the matter, seeking to find out why the proposed line was so delayed and proceeded to seek Light Railway powers themselves in 1914. The outbreak of the war forced matters into limbo, but with the conclusion of hostilities interest was revived. A public enquiry was held by the Light Railway Commissioners at Caernarfon on the 18th October 1921 and it was stated that a joint committee had existed in 1914 called the Portmadoc, Beddgelert and Caernarfon Light Railway Committee, appointed by the following local authorities; The Caernafon County Council. The Caernarfon Town Council, The Caernarfon Harbour Trust, The Portmadoc U.D.C. (Then known as the Ynyscynhaiarn U.D.C.), and the Rural District Councils of Glaslyn and Gwyrfai. This Committee applied in November 1914 and again in November 1921, for an order to revive old powers and to incorporate a new Company to run the proposed line, to be known as the Welsh Highland Light Railway Company. It was stated that the North Wales Narrow Gauge was then (1921) only carrying goods and the Croesor Tramway carried only goods and those by horse-power. No construction had been done between Dinas and Caernarfon but the P.B. & S.S. had acquired a substantial area of land from the Caernarfon Harbour Trust. The P.B. & S.S. and the North Wales Narrow Gauge had both offered to sell their undertakings, so the way was clear for the new Company to provide the through route.

A report from Major G.C. Spring on the North Wales Narrow Gauge virtually condemned the track. The main line, except for a short section before South Snowdon, was unfit for passenger working and required 300 new sleepers per mile. Timber on the bridges had rotted away. Bryngwyn station was unfit to take locomotives and the incline rope here was dangerously weak and only three wagons could descend at a time "Russell" was reported as being in good condition, capable of hauling a train of nine coaches. "Moel Tryfan", although fit to haul substantially less, was also described as being in good condition. The coaching stock, unused since 1916, stood idle in the yard at Dinas Junction, slowly deteriorating.

Spring also reported on the Croesor Tramway which, although purchased by the P.B. & S.S., had not undergone any work to bring it up to the required standard for steam haulage and passenger traffic (Although the P.B. & S.S. had claimed it had). Indeed, because of the light weight of the goods moved it appears that little work other than the most necessary maintenance had been carried out since it was laid. His report stated that the track was still of the original cast iron material and most of the sleepers were rotten. Pointwork was described as primitive, of quarry type, and without switch blades. The bridge adjacent to the road over the River Glaslyn at Pont Croesor was very faulty.

Had not the various local authorities taken a hand it is likely that the North Wales Narrow Gauge would have died within a few years although it is possible the Croesor Tramway, horse drawn and therefore of low running cost, might have survived. However the local authorities did exercise their not inconsiderable muscle, and the result was the Welsh Highland Railway.

CHAPTER TWO
THE WELSH HIGHLAND RAILWAY

Soon after opening in 1923 MOEL TRYFAN's crew take advantage of the stop at Beddgelert to clean out the smokebox. (W.H.R. collection)

The outcome of the enquiry was the incorporation on the 30th March 1922 of a new company under the Light Railways Acts of 1896 and 1912 called the Welsh Highland Railway (Light Railway) Company. It acquired from the 1st January 1922 the undertakings of the North Wales Narrow Gauge Railways and The Portmadoc, Beddgelert & South Snowdon Railway Company together with the powers of these companies relating to the building of railways between Caernarfon and Portmadoc. The authorised capital of the Company was £120,000 but only £90,000 was issued, fully paid, to the two undertakings acquired, in lieu of purchase money: £40,000 to the North Wales Narrow Gauge Railways and £50,000 to the Portmadoc, Beddgelert & South Snowdon Railway Company. No dividend was ever paid on these shares.

The Government agreed to subscribe an amount to the debenture stock of the Company equal to half the cost of completing the railway between Dinas and Portmadoc, providing the sum advanced did not exceed £37,500. The Ministry of Transport duly advanced £35,774 to the Company. It was stipulated that the Company could not raise more than a total of £175,000 in share and loan capital without the Ministers consent. Local authorities contracted to take debenture stock in the Company as follows:- Caernarfon County Council £15,000; Caernarfon

In early Welsh Highland days Festiniog locos were often used. JAMES SPOONER and train pose for the camera at Beddgelert about 1924. (A.Neale collection)

Corporation £5,000 (In respect of the proposed line from Dinas to Caernarfon): Gwyrfai Rural District Council £5,000 (£2,000 of which was in respect of the Dinas-Caernarfon link); Glaslyn Rural District Council £3,000, Deudraeth Rural District Council £3,000 and Portmadoc Urban District Council £5,000. As the Dinas to Caernarfon link was never built the £7,000 for this section was never subscribed, but the remaining £29,000 was duly forthcoming.

In January 1922 the survey for the connecting section between Croesor Junction and South Snowdon was commenced by Sir Douglas Fox & Partners and the contract for the building of the line was given to Sir Robert McAlpine & Sons on the basis of their experience in railway work although theirs was not the lowest tender. The work was commenced in March 1922. Attention was first given to reconditioning the old North Wales Narrow Gauge Railways section between Dinas and South Snowdon and this was re-opened for passenger traffic on the 31st July 1922. Although initially planned, passenger services were never re-introduced on the Bryngwyn branch however and for the rest of the life of the railway this branch remained goods only. "Russell" was the mainstay of the services during 1922 and for the first six months of 1923, "Moel Tryfan" being only used in an emergency, being in need of urgent repairs. Work was then commenced on the new 8.1/4 mile linking section and in reconditioning the Croesor Tramway line between Portmadoc and Croesor Junction.

The track was relaid between Portmadoc and Croesor Junction to make it suitable for steam traction and the bridge at Pont Croesor, previously largely wooden construction, was replaced with a series of steel girder bridges. The original route planned by the P.B. & S.S. had involved a gradient of one in twenty eight on a three mile section between South Snowdon

The Festiniog Railway's George England 0-4-0ST were frequently used on Welsh Highland trains in the early years. LITTLE GIANT pauses at Beddgelert with a Dinas train about 1924.
(Locomotive Publishing Co.)

and Beddgelert. In order to ease these the Company sought and obtained an Amendment Order in February 1923 which gave it powers to abandon the partially constructed P.B. & S.S. route and to purchase land to reduce the gradient on this section to one in forty with curves of a minimum radius of three chains instead of the much tighter curves envisaged by the P.B. & S.S.

The linking section was completed early in May 1923 and a series of trial runs carried out. The first, on the 12th May 1923, consisted of a Ffestiniog Railways locomotive,"Palmerston", ten loaded slate wagons and a open toastrack coach to carry the W.H.R. directors and representatives of the contractors. Further test runs were carried out on the 15th, 19th and 22nd May prior to Ministry inspection on the 24th May 1923. The completed railway was officially opened for passenger traffic on the 1st June 1923.

The new railway was now faced with an acute shortage of locomotive power. Only "Russell" and "Moel Tryfan" remained from the North Wales Narrow Gauge days, and although these had been sufficient to maintain the reduced goods only traffic on the North Wales Narrow Gauge in its final years and even the re-introduced passenger service prior to the opening of the complete line, they were insufficient to handle the proposed volume of traffic on the new line. "Moel Tryfan" was out of service by November 1922 and in need of a complete overhaul before she could run again. Under these circumstances the W.H.R. considered the re-purchase of "Gowrie", the former North Wales Narrow Gauge locomotive, and an engineer from the Ffestiniog Railway was despatched to Wakes yard to inspect the engine. His report, possibly influenced by stories of her previous unreliability, was against the re-purchase however.

It became necessary to borrow Ffestiniog Railway

F.Frith & Co. commemorated the new Welsh Highland Railway with a series of postcards. The local coal merchant's one ton Ford 'T' truck was posed by the bookstall at a gleaming new Beddgelert Station.
(F.Frith & Co. Ltd.)

engines to make up for the shortage. Most of the passenger trains in 1923 were worked by the Ffestiniog's England locomotives although it was not unknown for the Double-Fairlie engines to work straight through from Blaenau to Dinas Junction. The loan of locomotives was not as unusual as it might at first appear. The Board of Directors of the Ffestiniog Railway at the time was Henry Jack, Chairman (Also Chairman of the W.H.R.), Sir John Stewart and Evan Davis. (Both also directors of the W.H.R.).

This locomotive crisis was partly relieved when Colonel Stephens, who had been appointed Locomotive Superintendent and Civil Engineer of the railway on the 1st April 1923 purchased Baldwin 590, built in March 1917, from Messrs E.W.Farrow & Sons of Spalding. This ex-war department locomotive was one of many Baldwins built for use on the Western front during the First World War. "590" had Walschaerts valve gear, square cased slide valves on the top of the cylinders and a large sand box. It had 8 x 12 inch cylinders, 2ft coupled wheels, a grate area of 5·6 square feet and a heating surface of 254·5 square feet. The total wheelbase was 12ft 2ins, and tank capacity of 496 gallons. The weight in working order was $14\frac{1}{2}$ tons and working pressure was 140lbs (Although this has been stated as 178 lbs). In fact it had scarcely been altered from the condition in which it worked the Military Light Railways in France. The locomotive was to prove unpopular in service, giving a rough ride and being very prone to slipping, She was mainly used as a spare engine, although she did haul passenger trains. She was more usually to be found, at least in the early days, at work on the Bryngwyn branch. "Moel Tryfan" was duly taken into Boston Lodge Works and after a complete overhaul, returned to service sometime after July 1923.

There was also a shortage of rolling stock and once again the deficiency was made up by the loan of

Welsh Highland Rly.

A Dinas bound train rumbles over Bryn-y-Felin bridge about 1927. (C.J.Keylock collection)

Ffestiniog stock. Six new open "toast-rack" carriages with light roofs of War Department design were acquired from Robert Hudson Ltd. of Leeds. In later years one of the original North Wales Narrow Gauge coaches was converted into a refreshment car, apparently around 1928, in an attempt to give the railway more appeal to the tourist.

Correspondence between Boston Lodge and Colonel Stephens reveals that all was not well with the Welsh Highland finances from the start. Economies were made with men being laid off at Dinas Junction and all repairs being carried out at Boston Lodge. Traffic on the new railway did not reach the projected figures and the person who took the blame for this was Henry Jack who resigned as Chairman with effect from the 1st November 1924 and was replaced by Colonel Stephens. His first actions were to have "Moel Tryfan" and "Russell" cut down in size to enable them to run on the Ffestiniog's more severe loading gauge to facilitate through working from Dinas to Blaenau. This was successful in the case of "Moel Tryfan" and the outward effect of having the cab roof lowered and the chimney reduced in size merely gave the engine a Ffestiniog appearance. Due to "Russell's" larger boiler however, the cut down was not a success and on a test run it stuck in the Moelwyn tunnel and had to be reversed out, never to try the route again.

With the failure to pay an ordinary dividend on the shares and with the Railway defaulting on debenture interest payments, a receiver was appointed in March 1927. The slate industry had declined and the amount of freight the railway carried was well below expectations whilst passenger traffic had never reached its projected figures due to the slow, infrequent and unattractively timed service. The timetable allowed two hours ten minutes for the through journey from Dinas to Porthmadog

In another Frith view RUSSELL (then in original unaltered state) enters Nantmor Station in 1923. (F.Frith & Co. Ltd.)

compared with a time of between a half and a third of that by road transport.

In 1929 "Russell" was in need of re-tyring and his wheels were sent to the Hunslet Engine Co. Ltd., but when the work was finished the financial state of the railway left the Welsh Highland unable to pay. "Russell" was to remain out of service for nearly two years until the County Council stepped in and paid the bill so that the wheels could be returned and "Russell" put back into service.

Various attempts at economies were made, each reducing further the appeal of the railway to the public. By 1931 passenger trains ran only on Mondays, Wednesday and Fridays and, reflecting on the fall off of the slate trade, goods trains ran only on Tuesdays and Thursdays. In 1933 a small halt was established at Portmadoc immediately to the north of the Cambrian Line. Here passengers had to alight and cross the Cambrian Line on foot into Porthmadoc New (1923) Station where a connecting service, provided by the Ffestiniog, would run them into Porthmadoc Harbour station. In this way the Welsh Highland trains could avoid crossing the Cambrian line and so save paying the expenses of manning and signalling the crossing.

In November 1933 the joint committee representing the local authorities with investment in the Company decided to ask the debenture holders to close the line. But the point was raised that the section between Portmadoc and Croesor Junction was essential if the hoped for resurgence of the slate trade happened for the quarries in the Croesor Valley. The suggestion was made that Portmadoc Urban District Council could take over this section of the line and the rest closed. Negotiations were attempted with numerous organisations ,including other railways. After prolonged negotiations an agreement was reached on the 1st July 1934 whereby the Welsh Highland Railway was leased to the Ffestiniog Railway at the nominal rent of one pound for the first six months and

Welsh Highland Rly.

The new original Portmadoc New Station in 1923 with the crossing over the G.W.R. beyond. (C.J.Keylock collection)

subsequently for a percentage of the traffic receipts.

The Ffestiniog immediately tried to brighten up the Welsh Highland Railway as part of a campaign to attract more passengers. Several stations were given facelifts with light green paint being applied to the stations at Dinas Junction South Snowdon (Rhyd-Ddu) and Beddgelert and the refreshment room at Dinas Junction being re-opened. The passenger coaches were painted a variety of colours - red, grey, pink, blue and green all being used. "Russell" emerged from Boston Lodge from repair painted a shade of light green and "590" displayed a new reddish-brown livery. Nantmor station was re-named "Aberglaslyn" and an employee taken on to meet each train at Beddgelert in Welsh National dress. 500 sleepers were bought second-hand from the L.M.S.R. and cut in half to provide 1000 narrow gauge sleepers for permanent way repairs. Advertising attempted to attract more holiday makers to make the "round trip" - running from the North West coast by standard gauge to Dinas then on the narrow gauge through to Blaenau Ffestiniog, and back to their starting point by standard gauge again. It was a brave attempt but one doomed to failure. In another desperate attempt to save money all the stations were closed and a conductor/guard travelling on the train dispensed tickets from the equivalent of a bus conductors ticket machine.

Four and then six trains ran daily in each direction with Beddgelert becoming something like a border town. There was little, if any, through running and trains from both Portmadoc and Dinas met here and then returned whence they had come, passengers having to change trains if their destinations were further north or south. Trains however, were not timetabled to arrive at Beddgelert at the same time and the difference in arrival times further increased travelling time and proved unpopular with the passengers. Since 1930 the line had catered for passengers only during the summer season and had run as goods only during the winter months. (In fact there had been an earlier winter closure of passenger services between 15th December 1924 and 30th January 1925. When the service was re-introduced it was on a Friday only basis - (Portmadoc Market day). The 1936 summer service duly ceased on the 26th September 1936, and passenger services were never resumed. Goods traffic continued, but this consisted of only one or two trips per week on the Bryngwyn branch and even these ceased on the 1st June 1937.

Early on the morning of June 19th 1937 "Russell" left Dinas Junction to collect all the Ffestiniog wagons on the Welsh Highland metals and deliver them to Portmadoc. After leaving these in the sidings behind the harbour he ran on to Boston Lodge to collect the Baldwin, which had been sent there for repair. "Russell" then propelled the Baldwin back to Harbour station and collected all the Welsh Highland wagons in the sidings there. Pushing the Baldwin and pulling the wagons,"Russell" proceeded to Beddgelert where more wagons were attached and the sorry train continued toward Dinas. At Hafod Ruffydd the overgrown track caused much slipping and the load proved too much. "Russell" was forced to return to Beddgelert, drop off the wagons, and try again. This time Dinas Junction was safely reached and the Baldwin pushed into the loco shed. The following week "Russell" returned to Beddgelert for the wagons that had been left behind and proceeded back to Dinas with them, stopping along the way to collect other wagons in sidings along the route. On his return to Dinas "Russell" was run into the loco shed in front of 590 where they were to remain undisturbed for nearly five years.

An enthusiast who visited the line early in 1939 wrote: "The Locomotive shed at Dinas has a gaping hole in the roof. Underneath, open to the weather, stands "Russell" in quite good condition and looking well in her light green paint and red buffers. Alongside is 4-6-0 No.590 painted dark red, but rusty and dirty. About 40 wagons lie in the sidings to the north of the passenger station, in various stages of decay and overgrown with weeds. The track between Dinas and

Tryfan Junction in 1924. PALMERSTON and train of Festiniog stock are en route for Dinas Junction. (L. &G.R.P.)

Welsh Highland Rly.

In 1928 the prototype Kerr Stuart diesel locomotive was given extensive trials on the W.H.R. and is seen during a pause in shunting at Dinas Junction. The locomotive survives today in Mauritius..
(W.H.R. collection)

Tryfan Junction is well preserved, although much overgrown".

How long the railway might have lain, rusting quietly away, is anyone's guess but the outbreak of war and the resulting acute metal shortage brought action from the Ministry of Supply who, in 1941, requisitioned the metals for £1280 to assist the war effort. All the surviving equipment, with the exception of "Russell" was purchased as scrap by George Cohen, Sons & Co. Ltd., in July 1941. The nameplates, number plates and work plates of "Russell" and Baldwin "590" were sent to the York Railway Museum, where they can be seen today, at the instigation of Mr. V. Boyd-Carpenter.

The demolition contractors arrived at Dinas Junction in August 1941 and the undergrowth cleared in the cutting at Dinas. On August 11th a petrol tractor and observation coach started out but broke down near the carriage sheds. The following day another attempt was made and the train reached a point just beyond Tryfan Junction but had to return to Dinas due to the danger of overhanging branches breaking the glass of the observation coach. The following day a train consisting of the petrol tractor, a bogie flat wagon and four wheeled wagon set off again. All the level crossings had to be dug out along the way due to the danger of derailment, and Home Guard barricades had to be dismantled at Plas-y-Nant and in the Aberglaslyn tunnel. After dismantling the latter the train again returned to Dinas and the next day was successful in running through to Portmadoc New (1933) Station. This was as far as the train could

Despite its reputation for rough riding the Baldwin 4-6-0T 590 was a regular performer on the Welsh Highland. It was photographed taking water at Beddgelert on a typical Welsh 'soft day' some time in the mid 1930's.
(W.H.R. collection)

go as the crossing over the Cambrian line at Portmadoc had been taken out in October 1938 and the crossing box removed at the same time. The line was cut at South Snowdon and worked in two parts, being dismantled towards Portmadoc on the Southern half and to Dinas Junction on the northern end. The rails between Croesor Junction and Portmadoc (In the expectation of the re-opening of the Croesor Valley quarries after the war) and between Hafod Ruffydd and Pitts Head (For use, with moving targets, by the army for gunnery practice), were left insitu. When the Croesor Valley Quarries failed to re-open after the war the Croesor Junction to Porthmadoc section was lifted in 1948. At the same time much of the Hafod Ruffydd to Pitts Head section was also lifted although the Ffestiniog Railway recovered track from this area in the late 1950's.

All the girder bridges, with the exception of Pont Croesor (Which was dismantled) were left intact. Station buildings on the former North Wales Narrow Gauge section, all of stone construction but by then largely derelict, were left standing but the Welsh Highland corrugated iron buildings were dismantled with the exception of Porthmadoc New (1923) Station. In June 1942 an auction of rolling stock was held at Dinas. Baldwin 590 was cut up there outside the loco shed in August 1942 and "Russell" was sent by the Ministry of Supply to Brymbo Steel Works near Wrexham, for overhaul before working on their ironstone quarries at Hook Norton in Oxfordshire. Several of the carriages were purchased by local people and could be seen dotted around the hillsides for years afterwards. Two of these recently came into the hands of the Welsh Highland Light Railway (1964) Ltd. - the observation car, known as the Gladstone coach because it was once used by that Prime Minister and the former refreshment coach - which are currently under restoration.

The cut down RUSSELL pauses with her driver at Beddgelert.
(W.H.R. collection)

Prior to the demolition a suggestion appeared in "The Modern Tramway" magazine. Could not the line be saved and used to carry timber and slate and perhaps even passengers, therefore saving on buses and petrol, both scarce during the early years of the war? Another correspondent suggested in February 1941 that the line be taken over by an enthusiast organisation. An interesting if impractical suggestion in wartime but one which, if it had been adopted would have preceded the Talyllyn and the start of the preservation movement by more than a decade. A third correspondent expressed the hope that "Efforts would be made to re-open this necessary and picturesque railway and that such efforts will be crowned with success".

In March 1941 the Ministry of Transport replied that they understood that the Welsh Highland had been operating at a loss since its opening in 1923 and that there was no prospect of attracting sufficient traffic to the line to warrant its re-opening. The operation of the railway at a loss could not be justified on grounds of local public need and therefore no useful purpose would be served in pursuing the matter at the present time.

The Liverpool & District Federation of the Ramblers Association prepared an appeal which was sent to the local councils in November 1942 asking that the trackbed be converted to a long distance footpath, pointing out the success that the conversion of the former Leek and Manifold Narrow Gauge Railway track into a footpath had had. They had not done groundwork properly however, and had not realised that the section of the track between Hafod Ruffydd and Pitts Head was in use by the Army, and that the Croesor Junction to Porthmadoc section was still intact, hopefully to be opened at the end of the war, and so this scheme failed too.

Meanwhile the Ffestiniog Railway were left in an

The Welsh Highland demolition train in August 1941.
(W.H.R. collection)

unusual position. They still held a lease on the Welsh Highland Railway, which they had been trying to renounce since before the last train. It was not until the 4th November 1942 that they were able to get a Court Order cancelling the lease on the basis that they could not run a service on a line that had been demolished.

The Welsh Highland Railway had lasted just fourteen years. The main reason was that although conceived early it was executed too late to gain a foothold with the public. By the time it was finally opened Road transport was gaining the ascendancy and the slate industry diminishing, its product being replaced by roof tiles on new buildings. But it was not to die, however, for an enthusiasts group, inspired by the success of the preservation movement with the Talyllyn Railway, would be formed with the intention of restoring as much as possible of the glory of the former Railway.

Welsh Highland Rly.

CHAPTER THREE
THE ROUTE DESCRIBED

A view through the road overbridge into Dinas yard, 8th August 1935. (Late H.F.Wheeler)

Dinas Junction is situated on the former Bangor to Afon Wen branch of the L.N.W.R. Railway which like the Welsh Highland has now had its track lifted and the trackbed is now in use as a road, a cyclepath and medium distance walk, with other parts either built over (As with Chwilog station site) or left to grow wild. At the north end of the station stood the goods shed and the trans-shipment sidings. The passenger station lay between the standard and narrow gauge lines and consisted of a wooden refreshment room, a stone built station building and a small wooden hut which served as a booking office. As befitted its importance a station master's house was also built. An overbridge carried a minor road across the lines of both companies at the south end of the station and to the south of this bridge were the narrow gauge locomotive and carriage sheds, a water tower and a signalbox. The overbridge still stands today and visitors can look down on the site today from the bridge onto the current scene of industrial activity.

Leaving Dinas in a southerly direction, the line swung to the left into a cutting and passed under the main Caernarfon - Pwhelli road, the cutting on the south side of the road having been filled in as recently as 1989. Climbing at 1 in 47 through open countryside the line crossed the Gwyrfai, as mall stream, on a wrought iron girder bridge and passed under two minor roads whilst crossing the Gwyrfai twice more before reaching Tryfan Junction (2 miles). Here there was a passing loop, a wooden signal box and a station building of stone construction. It is worth noting here that all the station buildings on the Old North Wales Narrow Gauge part of the line were of stone construction, representing the optimism under which the line was built. In contrast all the buildings on the new section of the line south of South Snowdon Station and on the former Croesor Tramway section were all of corrugated iron or even more temporary construction, possibly reflecting the more cautious feeling prevailing at the time the Welsh Highland Railway was built.

The Bryngwyn branch immediately diverged to the right of the main line and turned though 180 degrees to run behind the station and back in the opposite direction to the main line. The gradient of this section started as 1 in 39 but eased down to 1 in 49 as Rhostryfan Station (¾ mile) was reached. The station consisted of a stone station building, a signalbox and one siding with a goods shed at its end.

Leaving the station the line entered a cutting and then crossed a small stream before passing under the Main road through the village and within 50 yards crossed a minor road on the level to head up through open countryside once again on slight embankments and cuttings to enable it to use the natural contours of the hill. The line then crossed the Bryngwyn Road on the level and immediately the gradient becomes 1 in 39 as it entered another cutting on a 180 degree curve emerging on an embankment. It then curved back the other way, round Bryngwyn Farm, and crossed the Bryngwyn Road again on the level. Immediately across the road lay Bryngwyn Station (2 ¼ miles). Here there was a signal box beside the level crossing gates, a stone station building, a goods shed, water tower, a run around loop and a siding. The station was dominated by the incline which was the real purpose of the branch. Set away from the station but with its own siding stood a Water Powered Slate Mill.

This slate mill has been variously incorrectly described as an explosives store and the reservoir built to feed the wheel has been attributed as being built to

Bryngwyn Station, with coal and empty slate wagons awaiting haulage up the quarry incline in the background. (C.J.Keylock collection)

Welsh Highland Rly.

A small group of passengers look thoroughly fed up with their enforced wait at Beddgelert. The lengthy pause each train made here was one more factor that drove passengers away from the Welsh Highland.
(W.H.R. collection)

feed the water tower. In fact the immediate area has a history of Water Powered Slate Mills. About two-thirds of the way up the incline, after it has crossed a minor road on the level, stand two cottages at a spot known as Glan Dwr. To the East of these cottages stood a large mill about which little is known except that it belonged to the Moel Tryfan Quarry and must have fallen into disuse sometime during the period 1870/90. In 1873, when the Moel Tryfan Quarry was advertised for sale it is described in the Auction details thus "The machinery for the sawing and planing of Slabs... are worked by a waterwheel thirty feet in diameter and three feet breast". When this Mill fell into disuse a much smaller mill was built and worked in the back garden of the cottage nearest the incline, allegedly by a Quarry worker who lived there. This worked until the late 1930's and was only demolished in comparatively recent times.

The incline was of double track and rose from 650 ft above sea level to 895ft over its half mile length. Unlike most similar Railways the Welsh Highland owned the incline up to the drumhead and the private tramways did not start until beyond that point. Here four branches converged, leading off to the Alexandra Slate Quarry, The Moel Tryfan Slate Quarry, The Fron Slate Quarry and the Braich Slate Quarry. Curiously a siding was built in the late 1920's leading across the Main Road the incline passed under and extending some 200 yards parallel to the incline. This however had a short life and was soon lifted as the gradient, being similar to the incline, proved too much for the Loco's serving it. Looking back from the top of the incline Dinas, the lines starting point, could be seen, some two miles away. The line had covered over twice that distance in reaching here.

Back at Tryfan Junction the main line climbed away

RUSSELL and train are seen leaving Bryn-y-Felin bridge for Aberglaslyn Pass in 1924. (F.Frith & Co. Ltd.)

at a gradient of 1 in 690 curving towards the east and passing under a minor road before running on a high embankment to reach the summit of this section and then starting to descend at 1 in 200 into the Gwyrfai Valley, running on a shelf on the valley side with the Afon Gwyrfai coming ever closer to the line as it descended. The line now passed under the Caernarfon to Beddgelert road and into Waenfawr station. (3¾ miles). Here there was another stone station building, a passing loop and sidings and a short branch line to a granite quarry. There was also a signal box, not used in Welsh Highland days but dating back to its North Wales Narrow Gauge predecessor.

The line continued alongside the main road, on a gentle climb of 1 in 150, and reached Bettws Garmon station (4 ½ miles) where there was the obligatory stone station building which still stands today, although derelict, a passing loop and a siding which crossed the Caernarfon to Beddgelert Road on the level to the left of the station and ran across the fields to serve the Ty Coch Slate quarries. About 50 yards after leaving the station the line crossed the Afon Gwyrfai on a 50ft span girder bridge and passed under the main road again. The line ran over open country again with the mountains slowly closing in. The Afon Gwyrfai was crossed again on another 50ft span girder bridge and the line now ran in close proximity to both road and river to reach Salem Halt. (5 ½ miles). Here a simple wooden hut was provided for passengers. The line now climbed at 1 in 120, increasing to 1 in 84 on a shelf above the river which was supported by a stone wall. From the right a small siding from the railways ballast pit at Salem Quarry joined another 50ft girderbridge to reach Plas-y-Nant Halt. (6 miles). Here there were no passenger facilities at all and little to show that the halt existed but for a short platform a gate in the wall on the main road and a path along the river bank.

The line then continued on an embankment towards Lake Quellyn, leaving the river bank and swinging left

Welsh Highland Rly.

RUSSELL and train for Portmadoc near Tryfan Junction. (W.H.R. collection)

through a shallow cutting and passing under the main road again. Here a wide, shallow cutting denoted the site of the first temporary terminus of the North Wales Narrow Gauge in 1877. The line then climbs at 1 in 67 following the contours of the land above the lake until it reached Quellyn Lake, latterly Snowdon Ranger, station (7 ¼ miles). Here there was a small stone station building, today converted into a cottage, a water tower and a siding. Below it, alongside the road, stood the former Snowdon Ranger Hotel from which it eventually took its name, today in use as a youth hostel.

The line continued to climb and crossed the Afon Treweunydd gorge on an impressive 100ft span girder bridge, 58 feet above the river. After a cutting the line ran along a shelf supported by a high stone wall to reach Glanrafon sidings (8 miles). These served the Glanrafon Slate Quarry which closed during the First World War. Here an incline with double tracks ran down at right angles to the main line with a weighbridge at the bottom of the incline and several sidings for the storage of slate wagons until they were collected by the railway. After a series of sinuous curves, climbing at 1 in 47, the railway traversed a sharp reverse curve to enter South Snowdon (Also known as Snowdon or Rhyd-Ddu during the life of the railway) Station. (9 ¼ miles). As befitted what was once the terminus of the North Wales Narrow Gauge, the brick and stone station buildings (Part of one serving as a signal box) were somewhat larger than those on the rest of the line and there was also a wooden refreshment hut and a goods shed, a long passing loop and two sidings. From the site of the station, 626 feet above sea level, an extensive panorama of mountain scenery can be observed, the summit of Snowdon, 3 ¼ miles distant, standing out prominently with the mountain rack railway train from Llanberis to be seen making its ascent on a clear day. The station site today is a car park provided for those who wish to walk up the Rhyd-Ddu track to the top of Snowdon - in a strange way almost retaining part of its former purpose, as a put down place for railway passengers wishing to attempt the same walk.

Climbing again at 1 in 100 and then 1 in 50, the line followed the road to Pitts Head Halt. (10 ¼ miles) the summit of the line at 647 feet above sea level. The line then passed under the road and commenced the long decent at 1in 40, following the hillside in a series of curves, passing Hafod Ruffydd Halt (12 ¼ miles) and shortly afterwards curving anti-clockwise to bring it back below Hafod Ruffydd. The line now ran back across open countryside as though it was returning to Rhyd-Ddu before entering another 180 degree curve which started with a cutting and ended on a high embankment above the Afon Colwyn on its left. Falling at a 1in 40 and carried partly through cuttings, partly on embankments the line crossed the Afon Meillionen and shortly afterwards entered a deep cutting. Leaving this the track curved again on a high embankment and there followed a shallow cutting in which the line crossed the Afon Cwm-Gloch again before curving left again and after crossing the Afon Cwm-Gloch again for the third time entered Beddgelert Station. (13 ¾ miles) In this latter section there are many sections of the Porthmadoc, Beddgelert and South Snowdon Railway works, unused when the Welsh Highland Railway was built, which can cause considerable confusion to anyone trying to trace the route. Indeed there appears to be two lines entering Beddgelert station.

Beddgelert Station was well equipped with a long passing loop and three sidings. The Station building and the goods shed were of corrugated iron construction and there was a water tower, still visible today from the car park below the station site, a small hut used as a store and one of the sidings had a short inspection pit. The rail to be found in the station site is not however remnants of the original track forgotten by the demolition teams but results of a tracklaying exercise by the Welsh Highland Light Railway (1964) Ltd. in 1973 and consists of rail lifted from the old Croesor Tramway in the Croesor Valley. The object of this tracklaying was to establish a "presence" in the area.

Leaving the station, the line continued to descend at 1 in 40, passing through a cutting into a 47 yard long tunnel at the rear of the Royal Goat Hotel. It emerged on an embankment alongside the Beddgelert to Tremadoc road and here the Porthmadoc, Beddgelert and South Snowdon intended to curve the line to the left and take it across the overbridge and along the embankment which would fall away to cross the river. The embankment was only partially built and the strange stone constructions along its line to the river would have formed an underbridge to provide the farmer, who's land the embankment would have crossed, with a means of getting from one part of his land to the other.

The actual course taken continued alongside the road gradually losing height until the line passed under the road where the road bends and immediately crossed the Afon Glaslyn at Bryn-y-Felin on a 75ft span steel lattice girder bridge. The line curved sharply and now ran alongside the river, climbing up above it at 1 in 80 on an embankment and through two short tunnels of 37 yards and 17 yards to emerge on a ledge high above the river which commanded a magnificent view of the Aberglaslyn Pass. The line then entered the 300 yard long Aberglaslyn tunnel. It is interesting to note that all three of these tunnels were built to standard gauge dimensions. Emerging from the tunnel the line crossed a high embankment into a rock cutting and crossed the Nantmor road on the level to reach Nantmor Station. (15 ½ miles). Here there was a short siding and a corrugated iron Passenger shelter.

The line then continued on a shelf above the Llanfrothen road, descending at 1 in 40 before passing through a cutting and crossing the Llanfrothen road by a steel girder bridge. Continuing on an embankment the line fell at 1 in 50, then 1in 250 to reach Hafod-y-Llyn Halt. (16 ¼ miles). A wooded area was then skirted before the line crossed the Afon Nantmor on a 75ft lattice girder bridge to reach Hafod Garregog Halt. (17 ¼ miles), where an old railway carriage was provided to act as a passenger shelter. Almost immediately after the halt the Afon Dylif was crossed by another lattice girder bridge and after a straight stretch of about half a mile the line curved right to make a junction with the Croesor Tramway at Croesor Junction (18 miles) where another old railway carriage served as a shelter.

The line then continued to Ynysfor Halt, (18 ½ miles) where there was a short siding and two small huts of timber and zinc, and then ran parallel to and

Welsh Highland Rly.

When the Festiniog Railway leased the W.H.R. in 1934 they immediately took steps to smarten up the Welsh Highland. A newly painted RUSSELL pauses by Portmadoc Harbour Station goods shed.
(W.H.R. collection)

along side the Llanfrothen Prenteg road on a low embankment until the Afon Glaslyn was reached. Here a water tank mounted on sleepers stood. The line then crossed the Afon Glaslyn on a steel girder bridge of eight 24 foot spans on masonry piers (which still stand alongside the road bridge today) and immediately crossed the road on the level to enter Pont Croesor Halt, (19 ¾ miles) where another small hut of timber and zinc was provided for passengers.

The line then ran across the flat lands of the estuary on a low embankment, crossing a minor road on the level, running past Pen-y-Mount and alongside Beddgelert Sidings where a trans-shipment bay was provided with the standard gauge. It is at Beddgelert sidings that the Welsh Highland Light Railway (1964) Ltd. have made their base and run their present services whilst preparing to head northwards along the old track as soon as the trackbed can be acquired.

Porthmadoc New (1933) station (21 miles) was then reached, which had a simple corrugated iron shelter. The line then crossed the Cambrian Coast line on the level and ran onto an embankment to reach Porthmadoc New (1923) Station (21 ¼ miles). The corrugated iron station building (still standing today although in ruins) and wooden refreshment room were situated in a field below the embankment. There was also a lengthy crossing loop and a water tower's concrete support still stands today. This was the terminus of the Welsh Highland Railway passenger services, unless you happened to be on a train running through onto the Ffestiniog Railway.

Leaving Porthmadoc New (1923) Station and still on the embankment the line crossed Y Cyt by a stone bridge and passed a flour mill (nowadays Portmadoc Pottery) on the left where there was a short siding and covered loading platform .Beyond this point another

RUSSELL and train head out of Portmadoc over the G.W.R. crossing about 1935. (W.H.R. collection)

siding on the right, running over what had previously been the Gorseddau Tramway, joined the line at the spot where the Gorseddau and Croesor Tramways had linked, running from a slate works. The line then crossed Snowdon Street on the level and made a wide curve passing the Glaslyn Foundry and entering Madoc Street. Here the line split. To the left the line crossed the High Street on the level and continued over the Britannia Bridge and into Portmadoc Harbour Station. (22 miles from Dinas Junction). This portion of the line was Ffestiniog Railway property however. To the right it crossed the High Road, again on the level, and entered the slate wharves alongside the Harbour.

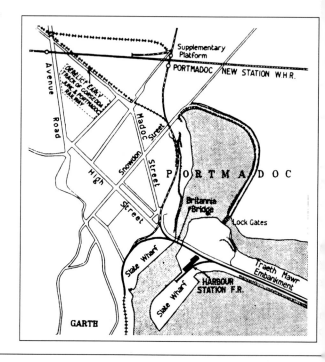

CHAPTER FOUR
WORKING THE LINE - A MEMOIR

*A busy scene at Portmadoc Harbour Station about 1935.
(W.H.R.collection)*

The following account of working on the North Wales Narrow Gauge Railway was written nearly 50 years ago by John Hughes, who worked for both the NWNGR and the WHR. Translated from the original Welsh by Mrs Myfanwy Roberts, the wife of former WHR driver Goronwy Roberts. It is an interesting memory of times past.

It's sad to think that only the old trackbed and ruins of the old stations remain of the 'Small Line' as we used to call it as children, as did our elders.

It's also odd to think and cast a glance back to find that there is almost none of the old workers still alive today. It was started about 1870 or soon after, A long time was taken to complete it. It was finished early in 1876. The railroad to Rhyd-Ddu was open before that. My grandfather used to say that most of the craftsmen were "Cornish" (Welsh Cornwall), building the trackbed, setting the tracks and most importantly building many bridges over rivers and under roads. Bridges built by them are still strong today. The only one not used today is Wernlasddu bridge which was built by the County Council some years ago to help the buses when they came to the area. Starting on the history, as it was at Dinas (Dinas Junction), a junction with the LMS Railway, there were many large sheds and store rooms to take goods to be delivered and also re-loaded to go with the small train. The big railroad

The Baldwin with a short train is about to enter the southern Aberglaslyn Tunnel on 8th. August, 1935. Note the ganger with his trolley roped on behind. (Late H.F.Wheeler)

wagons would come in one side, and the small line wagons on the other - the store had a long platform to enable unloading on the one side and loading on the other. Goods, flour and agricultural equipment used to come here. Coal was loaded from a siding the furthest end of the store. The Company had open wagons to carry 5 - 10 tons and closed to carry flour and goods. There were small wagons for slates, long trolleys which were used to carry iron bars or boilers to the quarries.

The quay for unloading slates is in the lower part of the station and there would be 3 or 4 doing the work of placing the slate wagons of the big line and T.R. Thomas, the foreman and checker who used to make a note of every broken slate.

There was an office for the station master and the clerk and a place for receiving new goods. The waiting room was a wooden building, as was the ticket office. Close by was a smithy's foundry and carpenters room, a large signal box and a large shed to keep carriages.

Let's cast an eye at the old workers. Lloyd, the old carpenter from town, William Owen, the blacksmith "Tyddyn Ganol", Brereton the fitter from Bontnewydd and some of the footplatemen. The most famous footplate men were John Williams (Jack Pen Bont or Lino Bach - his clothes were always shining with oil, he was a very funny, witty man), Huw Roberts (Huw Gath) who wouldn't go to Bryngwyn too often - too dry for his liking, William Hugh, a relative of Garreg Gath, a bachelor who would try to make a date with some of the visitors.

Another footplate man on the small line was W Hughes, Maen Coch. The only one still alive today is the guard. And we remember a porter who used to call himself Twm Cale - you would have to mind your hands and clothes in case he closed the doors on them. I remember one funny incident, Twm had turned the points the wrong way under the bridge to Saron and

Welsh Highland Rly.

RUSSELL looks very smart in her new Festiniog livery as she runs around the train at Beddgelert on 8th. August, 1935.
(The Late H.F. Wheeler)

the carriages overturned. The Station Master and others came running and Cale shouted "I'll pay for the damage Mr North, but not to any blooming quarrymen".

Let's look at the Station Masters and Clerks. Mr Tanner was one of the first ones and he built the house called "Fern Villa". Tanner would frequently be up in Bryngwyn and he had a handy trolley to come back on, a small four wheeled carriage with a long hand brake, which was pulled by the train on the way up. Following him came Mr North, another Englishman, and he didn't leave the station very often, other than to visit the "Ring", (The Mount Pleasant Pub). It was for him that the Company built the house owned by the small line today. After North's death came Danial Jones who was promoted from clerk and Guard to become Station Master, a bad tempered chap. John Jones, Bontnewydd, was one of the first clerks, then John Morris and Twm Morris, Guard and Danial,. Maggie, Danial's daughter, got his place when he was promoted.

Let's look at the guards, as they liked to call themselves, Twm Morris, "passenger train man" in his own words; Owen Morris, guard at Tyddyn Gwydd (Tryfan Junction) mostly, as Station Master there, who used to come on the trains to Rhostryfan and Bryngwyn, and back on the small trolley. (The same used by Tanner?) He kept many birds at Tyddyn Gwydd, very good singers all.

Robert Hughes, Station Master at Bryngwyn, we used to call Hughes Maen Coch. He was responsible for releasing the slate wagons on the big incline. Slates from Foel, Gors y Bryniau, Braich and Fron. Bryngwyn Station was important and busy when the quarries were at their peak. Hughes had a fatal accident one evening at the top of the incline. Dafydd Lloyd got his place and kept it for a number of years. Lets move on to the platelayers - Big Will Roberts, the foreman, Jeff Lamerick, Sion Williams, Saron, Sam Bach, Saron Sion Jones, Clochydd, Sam Jones (Chatam) and Ted from Llangfadlan and son in law Sion, Clochydd, and Thomas Ore.

Remembering the old engines - Tryfan Ranger, (Beddgelert), certainly one of the first, Snowdon Ranger, Moel Tryfan and the Russell, these last two used on the Rhyd-Ddu line (District).

We could say that the small line had a fairly secure track along the road - closed from animals. Excellent iron bars (Steel and iron) with 2 foot distance between each bar were along the line. The Company's Main Office was in Liverpool and Mr Dean was the last Manager. Now then, Mr Williams, lets take a trip from Dinas to Bryngwyn on the small train, leaving Dinas at 9.00am Tryfan Ranger is the engine, pulling two carriages - part of one is first class, then one closed big wagon carrying flour and goods, a large coal carrying wagon 16 small wagons and a guards van. We see the first class compartment is for the Moel Tryfan Company, and Mr Menzies for Gors y Brynniau and several other including two Jewish men who are making for the quarries to sell watches at Lunchtime. There's an old gentleman from Waen Wen selling ointment, excellent stuff for getting rid of… We take our seats and start off. We pass buildings - the smithy, carpenters shed, and the foundry, a signal box before going into Glanrhyd cutting and under the main Pwllheli and Portmadoc road bridge, coming very soon to the Pont Caer Moel bridge, - there is a kind of bridge under and over us at this point. Over the river and under the road from Rhos Isaf to the main road. There are many gates to be seen from the fields and stiles for footpaths. The train goes over a strong bridge at the bottom of Bodaden yard. Fencing encloses us to Wernlasddu bridge and Wernlas Ddu. Again under the Tir Caehen bridge and Bicall bridge before getting to Tyddyn Gwydd. At TyddynGwydd Station Owen Thomas puts small parcels in his office in the station from the train. There are two boarding for Bryngwyn. The guard attaches the trolley to the back of the train and off we go. We take the turning for the Rhostryfan and Bryngwyn Road, the other line going to Rhyd Ddu. Another bridge to go under, the road above going to various farms. By Caehen gates we stop, dew on the rail, and the fireman goes to sit on the front buffer of the engine to release sand on the rails - his job from here to Bryngwyn. The sand does its bit and we move on quite steadily. At Rhostryfan Station, we pass a signal box, one workers siding, a large waiting room, and a ticket office and goods depot. Rhostryfan Station is very convenient, almost in the village and also handy for Rhosgadfan. Many goods and things came to Rhostryfan Station, goods for Jones Hughes, Evan Griffiths, Bryn crin, and William Jones, Fourcrosses, with carriages to carry them away. A wooden building is by the station gate from the road to the school where there are scales for weighing carriages and platform machines. Starting off from Rhostryfan we see that there are coal wagons behind the station in the siding. Under a bridge from Dir Cae Rhug, then the old Wmffra bridge. In the village there is a road from Rhosgadfan crossing it. There are many gates from here on and many small bridges over streams, passing Ty Rallt and heading for Hen Dy Newydd. After this is an embankment and a strong bridge over the river at Caehaidd Bach Marshes. Caehaidd Terrace now comes into sight and we pass on to a large bridge to cross AfonWen. By now there is water from Ffynnon Wen, supplying hundreds of houses, a water pipe going as far as DinasDinlle and then a large cutting at Bryngwyn. A rather sharp turn and a strong river going under the track, with a strong bridge. The small train slows down there are many mountain ponies in the Station area, the guard goes to gather them ahead and steam from the whistle from old Penbont makes them gallop ahead. And here is Bryngwyn Station. We cross the road from Carmel with the gates closed across the road on both sides. We see a busy, important place.

The train provides an important service for neighbouring areas with the quarries bringing in most revenue. We find ourselves in an open space with many sidings, including a large coal siding. At Bryngwyn there is a signal box , an arms store, an office for Hughes (Station Master), a large waiting room next to the goods depot and also another large goods store and a high platform for unloading goods and flour. The coal siding is full and we see the following for a chat. Robert Thomas of Bryngwyn, John Roberts, Carmel, Evan Bwlchllyn, and Bob Siop of Fron. Everyone is busy. There is a carriage for Tomos Elias, who's coming for goods boxes. There is a similar weighing machine to Rhostryfan here, very busy at the foot of the incline. We are delivering a new engine for the Foel Quarry. This one had a special

Welsh Highland Rly.

The Welsh Highland's 590 and the Festiniog's TALIESIN await departure with their respective trains at Portmadoc Harbour, 8th. August, 1935. (The late H.F.Wheeler)

train to bring it up from Dinas. There is a great fuss, we're almost ready to start, it's attached to the wire rope and Hughes is at the top of the incline by the drum. He begins raising it slowly and after 100 yards it stops and after enquiring we find that the workers are moving in the engines way to go under the middle of Fronheulog bridge. It then went up successfully and the small Gors-y-Bryniau engine pulls it up to the Foel Road. The Gors engine is called Kathleen. There would be many accidents on the incline, couplings or axles snapping as they travelled at such speed, and all losses against the small line Company. Two trains daily to Bryngwyn, morning and afternoon. But on Saturday 4 or 5 trips. I can remember the first on Saturday at about 8.00am, they called it the market train. The last train would be at Bryngwyn at about 8pm or 9pm.

The stations were all in the same style as I mentioned earlier. Let's look again in general. Some things are never to be forgotten. Hughes, Bryngwyn Station Master, injured at the top of the incline, his leg almost cut off, seeing him on the ground and William Wern shielding him and carrying him on a ladder down to Bryngwyn with me helping to carry the ladder; after much delay reaching Bryngwyn to find that the engine and carriages and Dr Davis had come from Dinas but Hughes was placed in the van. Many lifts we had from him to the old Ty Newydd. Childhood memories of Rhostryfan Station- playing ball in the square, riding on the wagons by the station where William Sam broke his leg. One of the Post Office workers was collecting goods in a handcart with William loading at the back. The cargo tipped onto his legs, breaking one of them. The Bont Policeman coming to school when two of the wagons we were playing with ran away from us and ran down to Tyddyn Gwydd before coming off the rails. How would such a thing be dealt with today? (Children's

The Baldwin and train rumble across Portmadoc High Street at the start of the long slow journey to Dinas on 9th. August, 1935. (The late H.F. Wheeler)

Court?). Two from Rhostryfan had a hand in doing it. -I.T. Thomas, Fron Oleu, and Griff Roberts, Glan Corrog, who marshalled the carriages, he had a licence to do so. The point blades at Tyddyn Gwydd had to go to Penygroes Smithy to be treated. I.J. Thomas had a hand in finishing as well the process of getting rid of the iron rails. Many of the old stiles are still standing. Two wooden ones I think - an iron one by Hen Dy Newydd, a frail wooden one nearer to the Rhostryfan path at Pencae Clogwyn and an iron one opposite it - an iron one to Tir y Gaerwen, a gate instead of the old stile by the station and the same in the wild land at Bodgarad. A wooden stile by Henryd river, Tir Bodaden, two iron ones each side of Bodaden yard. Looking back again we try to remember those who last worked on it: - A blacksmith from Bryn Melyn, Daffydd Roberts, carpenter from Groeslon, Lloyd Dol Ellog, Robert Roberts, Glanrhyd, J Williams, Thomas Ore, Dinas, T.R. Thomas, Caradog Jones, Glanrhyd.

The small line was very convenient for the area, especially Carmel, Bwlch y llyn, Cesarea, when there was only carts to carry goods from Caernarfon or stations on the big line and very few carriages to carry people. The small train was in demand on Saturdays until the buses came. The end of the quarries proved to be the end for the line as well.

The small line from Tyddyn Gwydd to Bryngwyn ceased to operate in 1934 and everything finished in 1937. Isn't it sad to think that the rails were used to make shrapnel in the last war. Many parts of it have been choked and closed by thorns and brambles some parts make convenient footpaths for the farms and even though it's sad to think that the small line is finished, there are some things that remain to remind us of the good old days and many trips we had on it. Many things spring to mind in recalling our adventures on the line as we sit by the fireside."

Y Groeslon John R. Hughes (Crwydryn)

Today there are still many people in the area who can recall the "Little Line" running, and still yearn for its re-appearance. The Welsh Highland Railway Ltd. is dedicated to making these wishes come true.